Contents

It is strongly recommended that walkers have suitable clothing and footwear, appropriate to the walk and conditions that can sometimes be encountered on open moorland and exposed hillsides. This usually means walking boots, outer waterproof/windproof jacket and a type of walking trousers (not jeans) along with a warm sweater and other body clothing. A small day rucksack with some food/drink and your personal items is also strongly recommended.

The description of a route or track is not evidence of a right of way.
Any compass bearings shown in this book are given as magnetic bearings.

It is recommended that a compass and the following map are used in conjunction with these walks.
Ordnance Survey Explorer No. 278 Sheffield & Barnsley.
279 Doncaster, Conisbrough & Maltby for walk No. 6.

To help shorten the text the following abbreviations have been used throughout.
PF = Public Footpath   **LT = Left**
PB = Public Bridleway   **RT = Right**
CP = Car Park   **FB = Footbridge**

I do hope you enjoy this selection of walks, which are spread generally throughout the Sheffield and Rotherham boundaries. The majority are not too demanding, with the scenery and views on most walks, surprisingly excellent considering the short distance from the centre of each town and city. I hope you get as much pleasure from walking them as I did.
Brian Smailes

Walk 1: Tankersley Park & Old Hall Walk
Walk Time: 2hrs   Distance: 4.2miles/6.7Km
Start: St. Peters Church, Tankersley. GR. 349996

1. Descend Black Lane in front of the church towards the M1 motorway. You may see Tankersley Golf Club to your **RT.** Follow the lane through a subway under the M1 and round to farm buildings with the ruin of an old hall on your **LT.** Turn **LT** on the lane to pass the ruins and walk to the next bend.

2. Turn **LT** at the bend on a **PF** into woodland on the Timberland Trail. Your path soon joins another **PF** where you turn **RT** and continue up to the grounds of Bell Ground House. Look for a stile at the end of the line of trees ahead, cross then turn **RT** keeping the hedgerow on your **RT.**

3. At far end of field, follow it round anti-clockwise to a stile on the **RT,** leading through woodland for 100yds to the rear of an industrial area and cross a small **FB** there. Walk across the industrial area to a barrier, and as you go through, look for a **PF** and sign on your **RT** and follow this narrow old lane towards the M1 motorway.

4. Continue on this track to another track crossroads and walk straight across still heading towards the M1. Just before arriving at the embankment of the M1, cross a stile near a pond to take you along by the embankment.

5. Turn **RT** to cross a **FB** and stile alongside the embankment and walk to a short lane ahead with an underpass to the **LT,** which you go through to a metal stile leading onto the golf course.

6. Keep generally **LT** on the golf course, crossing between the greens and through a small coppice on bearing 191°M from the stile. Look for a **PF** sign on higher ground at the top **LT** corner of the 15th tee near the M1 to emerge near the roundabout on the A616.

7. At the main road turn **LT** for 30yds crossing to a **PF** sign by a metal gate and stile. Cross the stile, ascend then descend the field to an old tank parked at the entrance to an industrial estate. Cross the road behind the tank to the corner of unit 1, looking for a **PF** sign hidden behind trees just round the corner. This takes you along by a fence and unit 1.

8. You come to woodland where you turn **RT** on a path skirting the outer edge of the wood and behind the factory units on the industrial estate. At the far end of the last factory, the path descends into the wood. Follow the main path through the wood to eventually meet a wide track crossing **LT** to **RT.**

9. Turn **RT** to a **PF** sign a short distance away then **LT** on a distinct bridleway track running parallel with the A616, 150yds further over to your **RT.** Stay on this track for 760yds to a stile on your **RT** leading onto the A616. Cross the road with care to cross the stile opposite.

10. Ascend to a further stile and continue up the hillside to the topside of the golf course. There are good views of the High Green area from here. Descend the hillside over the fairway keeping a pine tree copse to your **RT** and looking for **PF** marker posts as you descend. Walk to a pylon at the lower **LT** corner of the course, bearing 50°M from the top of the hill near the pine trees.

11. Cross a stile to walk on the narrow path by a broken stone wall for 550yds, pass holly bushes as you walk back to St. Peters Church where you started.

A61

M1

A6135

† START

BELL
GROUND
HOUSE

A61

A616

PYLON

PINE
TREES

FIELD

RUIN

CROSS
ROAD
HERE

TRACK
CROSSROAD

A6135

A616

MINOR ROAD

MINOR
ROAD

M1

N

WALK 1
Not to Scale
**TANKERSLEY PARK
& OLD HALL**

Walk 2: Roman Ridge Walk
Walk Time: 2hrs 20mins   Distance: 5miles/8Km
Start: Memorial in Church St. Greasborough. GR. 418957

1. Park at the memorial then turn **LT** along the main road to The Milton Arms.
2. Turn **RT** opposite The Milton Arms following a sign on a narrow path called The Balk, descending to cross a **FB**. Continue straight ahead, ignoring the steps off to your **LT**.
3. Go through a kissing gate to ascend the **RT** side of a field. At the top **RT** corner; pass through into the next field, continuing to the main road at Nether Haugh.
4. At the main road cross with care onto a footpath at the far side then turn **LT,** walking for 660yds to a house on the **LT** at a sharp **RH** bend. Turn **LT** onto a track behind the house and continue for 160yds to another house on the **RT.**
5. A **PF** sign points **RT** alongside the house. Follow this for 130yds to an old stile at the entrance to a field where you walk diagonally across on bearing 266°M from the stile to the far **LT** corner. You come to another old stile with an arrow pointing diagonally **LT,** descending across the next field.
6. Follow the path down then over a **FB** and stile into a grass field. Take a bearing 260°M from the stile, walk diagonally **RT** to ascend to another stile.
7. Cross into another grass field then walk diagonally **LT,** crossing the Roman Ridge to emerge onto a lane. Turn **RT** walking for 280yds to a metal 5-bar gate on the **LT** then turn down a track descending to the ponds. Continue over the bridge between the two ponds, still on the track.
8. At the far side of the ponds where the path forks, take the **RT** fork to ascend on a track then a path between fields bearing 236°M towards Scholes Coppice.
9. You come to a small wood on your **RT** where you bear **LT** by the outside edge of the wood. As you ascend, look for a large wooden post then a broken fence line on an old track, walking towards a large wooded area at the far side of an open field known as Upper Common. Follow the track, which swings **RT** towards an opening through trees on the **LT** side. Walk through on a tarmac track to a main road beside flats.
10. Turn **LT** along Town Lane then on Church St. for ¾mile back to Greasbrough.

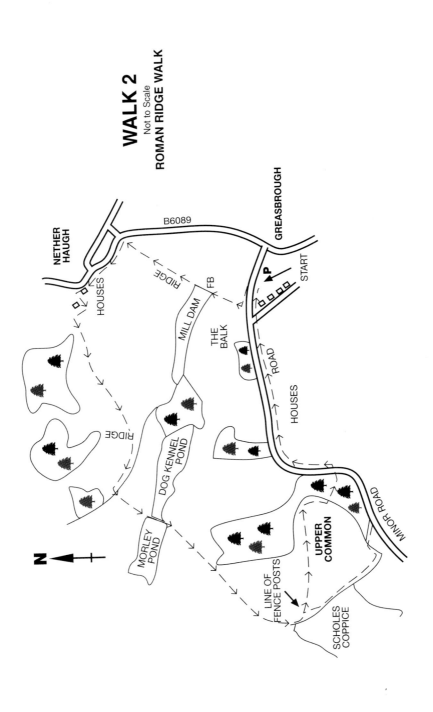

WALK 2
Not to Scale
ROMAN RIDGE WALK

NETHER HAUGH

B6089

GREASBROUGH

START

P

HOUSES

RIDGE

MILL DAM

FB

THE BALK

ROAD

HOUSES

RIDGE

DOG KENNEL POND

MORLEY POND

MINOR ROAD

LINE OF FENCE POSTS

UPPER COMMON

SCHOLES COPPICE

N

Walk 3: Whalejaw Hill Walk
Walk Time: 2hrs 15mins   Distance: 5miles/8Km
Start: Corner of Greno Knoll/Woodhead Road. GR. 323957

1. Park in an opening beside Greno Knoll. A **PF** sign by the road points into the wood, which you follow. The narrow path ascends by a wooden seat then descends to the **LT.** At a crossroads in the path by a marker post, carry straight ahead as you now walk near the edge of the wood towards Woodseats. You come to a clearing in the wood with a lane and a 5-bar gate on your **LT** but continue slightly **RT** at a marker post with a yellow arrow on it.

2. You start to ascend, going clockwise, then branch **LT** to come to another clearing. Bear **LT** here; do not take the ascending path to the **RT.** You now start to descend gradually. At the next open area carry straight on, still descending slightly. To your **RT** further on you see an open field surrounded by trees.

3. Continue ahead to a wooden 5-bar gate with an opening at the side. Go through and continue now on a wider path alongside a stone wall. You see another field on your **RT** with a large house at the far side at GR.333945. Continue on the wide path and you come to a 5-bar gate with an opening. Go through then where you see a **PF** to the **RT** and one straight ahead, take the one straight ahead along the back of the houses.

4. You come to a small housing estate but continue ahead on the narrow road known as Greno Gate, which is part of the Trans Pennine Trail. You emerge at The Old Red Lion Inn on Main St. Turn **LT** and continue for 1mile, passing the Angel Inn and the Community Centre on your **LT.**

5. At a crossroads with Saltbox Lane continue across onto Foxhill Road. Pass open fields to arrive at another estate and continue ahead to a farm on the **RT** called Shaw Hill Farm and a **PF** sign.

6. Ascend to another **PF** sign near the farm following it **LT** in front of the farm, ascending onto the hill then descending the overgrown path onto Edge Lane. Walk for 250yds to the top of Edge Lane and look for a **PF** sign just round the corner on the **RT,** which leads to Whalejaw Hill.

7. Follow the narrow ascending path along the ridge with good views to the **LT.** Continue on the narrow path keeping a stone wall on the **RT.** You emerge on a bend in the road on Whalejaw Hill GR.325934. Go straight across on the narrow path continuing to Prior Royd Wood

8. Turn **RT** on reaching the wood going over stone steps to ascend the **RT** side of the wood to the top corner. Bear **LT** over stone steps onto a PF through the wood. The path skirts just inside the wood then at a crossroads on the path, continue straight across through an opening in a fence.

9. Keep ahead then eventually the path joins with a road where you turn **LT** then **RT** after 100yds onto a **PF** passing an iron gate. You are now on a sandy path, when it forks, take the **LT** fork and carry on, ignoring paths off to the **RT.**

10. Pass a 'trig' point on **LT** and stay on this path to emerge near the seat where you started and turn **LT** to go back to your starting point.

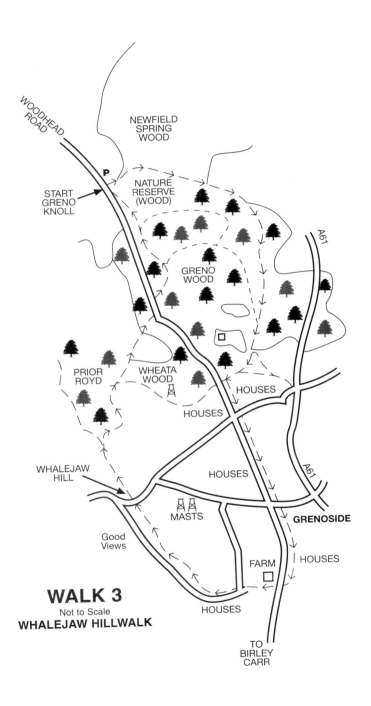

WOODHEAD ROAD

NEWFIELD SPRING WOOD

P

START GRENO KNOLL

NATURE RESERVE (WOOD)

A61

GRENO WOOD

PRIOR ROYD

WHEATA WOOD

HOUSES

HOUSES

HOUSES

HOUSES

WHALEJAW HILL

MASTS

Good Views

A61

GRENOSIDE

HOUSES

FARM

HOUSES

WALK 3
Not to Scale
WHALEJAW HILLWALK

TO BIRLEY CARR

Walk 4: Lakes/Canal Walk
Walk Time: 2hrs 5mins   Distance: 5.1miles/8.2Km
Start: Rother Valley Country Park, Visitors Car Park.
GR. 454828

1. From the visitor centre **CP** in Rother Valley Country Park, walk out of the **CP** and back over the bridge a short distance, crossing the River Rother.

2. At the far side of the bridge turn **LT** on a wide path towards Waleswood. Continue ahead past a metal suspension bridge keeping close by the course of the river. When you come to a stone bridge over the river near the railway, turn **LT** to cross it then **LT** again round the bottom of the railway **FB** to come onto a path round the lake.

3. Turn **RT** to walk in a southerly direction along the length of the lake, continuing to some metal 5-bar gates and a sign Trans Pennine Trail just over halfway along.

4. Turn **RT** walking away from the lake going under a railway bridge then **LT** on a path signposted Killamarsh. Continue straight ahead crossing a bridge over the main road to a sign pointing **RT** to Killamarsh shops.

5. Ascend the short stony path, crossing an iron **FB**. Go through a kissing gate onto a lane; turn **RT** then **LT** following a **PF** Cuckoo Way behind a newly built bungalow.

6. Follow this path by the old Chesterfield Canal. Cross a main road onto a grass area following the path round to rejoin the old canal further along. You eventually emerge onto Bridge St. then cross onto Kirkcroft Lane. A sign nearby points to the parish church.

7. Stay on Kirkcroft Lane until you reach the church then turn **LT** down Church Lane. Look for a footpath leading off **LT** to Nether Green and the country park 100yds below the church and before the bottom of the lane.

8. Follow the winding path to the main road 550yds further, walking between the houses in a NNW general direction.

9. On reaching the B6058 at Nether Green, cross onto another **PF,** which takes you again along the route of the old canal with three lakes of the country park on your **LT**. Continue in the same direction on the **PF** back towards the visitor centre.

10. On reaching the access road into the park, turn **LT** to take you back to the visitor centre.

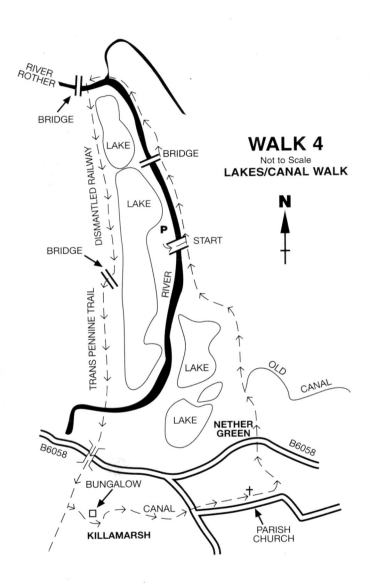

RIVER ROTHER

BRIDGE

LAKE

DISMANTLED RAILWAY

BRIDGE

LAKE

P

START

WALK 4
Not to Scale
LAKES/CANAL WALK

N

BRIDGE

TRANS PENNINE TRAIL

RIVER

LAKE

OLD

CANAL

LAKE

NETHER GREEN

B6058

B6058

BUNGALOW

CANAL

KILLAMARSH

PARISH CHURCH

Walk 5: Ringinglow/Hanging Water Walk
Walk Time: 4hrs   Distance: 5.7miles/9.2Km
Start: Outside the Norfolk Arms on Ringinglow Road.
GR. 291837

1. With the Norfolk Arms in front of you, turn **RT,** walking for 140yds past the telephone box to a **PF** sign on **LT.** Cross the stone steps to walk 310yds on a narrow, gradual descending path between a stone wall and a wire fence. Go through a small wooden gate then cross a narrow field to an opening in the stone wall opposite.

2. With good views of Sheffield off to the **RT**, descend a steep hill to a stile you see in the fence at the bottom. Cross then turn **RT** along Clough Lane (track). Continue walking parallel with Porter Brook for 2.2miles on a track/road/**PF.** The path follows the valley near the brook and you follow the **PB**/footpath signs or blue city centre signs

3. Your path emerges by a stone bridge where you cross, still by the brook. You come to a narrow stone bridge with ponds nearby. Do not cross but take the narrow footpath off to the **RT** by the fence line.

4. You come to some large stone built houses beside a sharp bend in the road. Just past the front of the houses, pass through a small wooden 5-bar gate and turn **RT** on the **PF** (not the Bridleway) to walk on a distinct path with the brook on your **RT.**

5. You pass a monument to Thomas Boulsover the inventor of Sheffield plate who died in 1788. Soon you pass some cottages to emerge on a road where a sign 'easy going trail' is on your **LT.** Follow this again by the brook, keeping it on your **LT.** At a stone bridge by a road, cross and continue as before to next road, which you cross.

6. You are now on a wide tarmac track, still nearby the brook. Further on you pass a stone building on your **LT** in the park area followed by two small **FBs** near each other. Cross the second one, walking to a wide expanse of water with houses on the far side. This area is known as Hanging Water.

7. Descend some steps on your **RT** and cross a small metal **FB** turning **LT** again on the main path. Approaching the main road ascend some steps on your **RT** leading to two bowling greens then turn **LT** round by a green hut and up to the **RT** to the tennis courts.

8. Turn **RT** just before the tennis courts then **LT** on a path through the wood. You may see your original path below on the **RT**. Continue on a gradual descent to 170yds before the bridge; bear **LT** to take you to the road at the far end of the row of houses on Highcliffe Rd.

9. Beside the sign for Highcliffe Rd, follow the **PF** sign beside it walking until you soon see a 4-way **PF** sign. Turn **LT,** following this path as it swings **LT.** Take second path off **RT** (do not walk to houses you may see ahead).

0. Look for a small wooden post with some arrows on it; bear **RT** to take you to some houses. Walk to the **RT** of the houses then **LT** between them. You emerge on a road, turning **RT** along a cul-de-sac onto a path descending to a farm and emerging onto a road.

1. You see Ivy Cottage Lane on the bend, where you turn **LT,** following the road round for 110yds. You arrive at the entrance of Sheffield Guide Assoc. Whitely Wood Outdoor Centre on **RT** and a **PB** sign pointing inside, which you follow. This winds round Common Lane open space. Follow path round **RT** side of field by a line of trees, emerging on a road with an old school house opposite by the side of a **PF.** Walk for 350yds on that **PF** to the main road.

2. Turn **RT** on Ringinglow Road keeping to the path at the side for 1260yds back to the Norfolk Arms.

Walk 6: Ravenfield Park Walk.

Walk Time: 2hrs 45mins   Distance: 6.2miles/10Km
Start: The Wapping (road) at Hooton Roberts. GR. 485970

1. From The Wapping, follow the lane round passing the houses. Near the end of the lane the road turns into a track. Continue on this track passing a barn. Where the lane stops, there are two fields, look for the **PF** between them and ascend through a thin line of woodland on a path 220yds to an open field on high ground.

2. Turn **RT**, walking along the **RT** side of the field where there are good views towards Rotherham. After 160yds you should see a diagonal track across the field bearing 147°M from the start of the track, which leads to Firsby Hall Farm.

3. Take this track, bearing **LT** round the farm buildings. Do not take the first **PF** sign on the **LT** but take the second, bearing **LT** by two stone posts. This leads up a long narrow field on a wide **PB**. Firsby Reservoir is below **RT**. At the top you come to an open field in front with telegraph lines overhead.

4. Take a bearing 127°M to walk by a line of posts across to a hedge and through an opening onto another **PB**. You may see the masts on Beacon Hill on your **LT**.

5. You are now on an old lane where you turn **RT,** descending to Firsby Brook, go through an old gate as you cross the brook. Walk up the **LT** side of a field between two wire fences. You emerge on a farm access track by a 5-bar gate, known as Park Lane.

6. Bear **LT** on Park Lane, walking for 990yds and passing Conisbrough Grange Farm to Moor Lane at Braithwell Common. Turn **RT,** walking now on Braithwell Road keeping on the grass verge for 875yds to Ravenfield Grange on the **RT** side just past the start of the houses.

7. Look for a stile next to a sign for a **PF** and Braithwell Gun Club. A pond is just inside the field. Cross the stile, bearing **LT** round the pond bearing 317°M for 820yds in a straight line crossing two stiles to emerge on a path between a line of trees. Continue to Arbour Lane, emerging on a bend.

8. Continue heading north on the tarmac lane for 765yds to an entrance into Ravenfield Park and a stile there next to a barrier. Cross the stile and bear **LT** at a map display board. Descend steps taking you to the ponds below. At the bottom of the steps is a fence line; keep **LT** alongside it to a **FB,** which goes over the ponds.

9. Do not cross the **FB** but take the path bearing **LT** and gradually ascend the hillside before descending to Hooton Brook beside a stone wall.

10. Walk now on a distinct path ascending for 440yds by the wall then up a flight of steps in woodland to another wall at the top with a field at the far side. Turn **LT** on a short narrow path to a wall, which you cross to continue to the side of the open field.

11. Turn **LT** on joining the field, walking along the edge to take you on your original route back to a small marker post pointing **LT,** where you turn back through the thin woodland on your original path, then **RT** at the bottom back into Hooton Roberts.

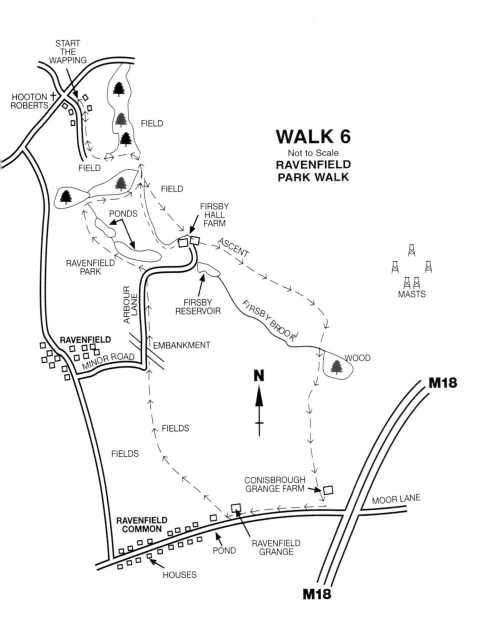

START
THE
WAPPING

HOOTON
ROBERTS

FIELD

FIELD

FIELD

WALK 6
Not to Scale
RAVENFIELD
PARK WALK

PONDS

FIRSBY
HALL
FARM

ASCENT

MASTS

RAVENFIELD
PARK

ARBOUR LANE

FIRSBY
RESERVOIR

FIRSBY BROOK

WOOD

RAVENFIELD

MINOR ROAD

EMBANKMENT

N

M18

FIELDS

FIELDS

CONISBROUGH
GRANGE FARM

MOOR LANE

RAVENFIELD
COMMON

POND

RAVENFIELD
GRANGE

HOUSES

M18

Walk 7: Ridgeway Walk
Walk Time: 3hrs 10mins   Distance: 6.4miles/10.3Km
Start: Ridgeway Craft Centre. GR. 403816

1. From Ridgeway Centre **CP** turn **LT** on the main road walking up the hill to the last bungalow on the **LT** where there is a **PF** at the far side of it next to a 5-bar gate. Turn **LT** here and walk along a narrow path and over a stile into a field.
2. Descend the field to the **RT** of a wood. Cross a stile and follow the narrow path to another stile. Descend the field to two stiles in a small copse, taking the **RT** one to emerge on an old lane, which you ascend. Follow the lane round to public toilets on a bend and The Bridge Inn on **LT**.
3. Continue straight on for 220yds to Geer Lane at Birleyhay off to the **RT**. Walk along it following the narrow road round between the houses and over the stream. At the next sharp bend, continue across following the arrow on a wooden marker post to ascend the hillside over a stile by a 5-bar gate.
4. Cross another stile in top corner and continue to far side of that field. As you approach Litfield Farm you emerge on an old lane where you turn **LT** to ascend as the lane narrows. Follow it into Ryalls wood then at a fork in the path bear **LT** descending a narrow path to the far side of the wood. The path passes over a ditch onto a track at GR. 390811.
5. Turn **LT** descending then ascending a farm track to Povey Farm. As you reach the farm look for a wooden signpost near the farm buildings then bear **LT** down a lane to the lower side of the farm. Continue to the fork in the lane then bear **RT** descending a stony lane to lower ground where you come to a **FB** and ford.
6. Cross the **FB**, turning immediately **RT** over another **FB** then **LT** up an old lane called Owler Car Lane. Look for a **PF** sign on **RT** pointing to the other part of Owler Car Lane, ignore that and continue to a small open area with two 5-bar gates higher up.
7. Turn **RT** over a stile there on a **PF** crossing a field; turn **LT** then **RT** to descend to a **FB** in a wood at the bottom at GR. 377803.
8. Cross the **FB** then ascend the path ahead to a wooden 5-bar gate and stile on your **LT**. At this point turn **RT** on a path leading to the **RT** side of Bridle Road Wood. Continue ascending the side of the wood in a northerly direction to a stile at the top as you leave the wood.
9. Cross the stile and walk directly ahead on a track on the **LT** side of the wood to the far corner then turn **RT** into the wood at GR. 377809. Cross a brook before ascending a path to the **LT** to an opening between two fields. Bear **LT** then **RT** to ascend the side of the **LT** field to the top emerging on Hazlehurst Lane.
10. Turn **LT** onto the lane, continuing to the access road to Mansion House Farm. Turn **LT** for 50yds then **RT** on a **PF** ascending a field (with two blocks of flats ahead) to join another **PF** on the far side crossing **LT/RT**.

11. On joining that path, turn **RT** towards Little Carterhall Wood. Follow that path over several fields to a lane; turn **RT** then **LT** following **PF** sign over a stile into next field.

12. The path swings **RT,** look for the walker sign on a wooden post then bear **LT** as you approach Little Carterhall Wood. Continue slightly **RT** then **LT** alongside a field. Look for a narrow opening near the wood in the far **LT** corner of the field.

13. Turn **LT** descending, then **RT** alongside the wood. Look for steps descending a path into the wood. Follow the path through the wood, over a **FB** then steeply up to the top at the far side. Look for a stile to **RT** of a metal 5-bar gate taking you past Carterhall Farm towards Robin Brook Lane.

14. Skirt the farm and at a stile next to a small 5-bar gate, cross then at an open area bear **RT** between hedges along the old Robin Brook Lane.

15. Cross another stile and **FB** ascending a hillside to a stone stile at the top. Bear **RT** between the fields then continue along a narrow path to pass between some new houses to the main road and the Ridgeway Centre **CP** opposite.

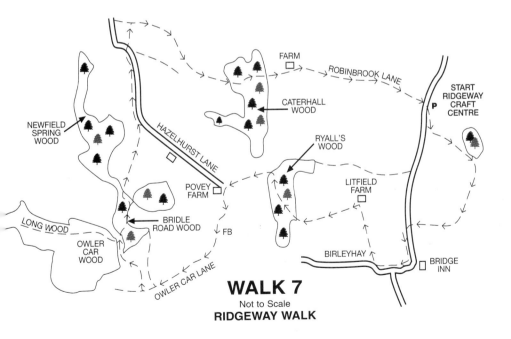

WALK 7

Not to Scale

RIDGEWAY WALK

Walk 8: Houndkirk Hill Walk
Walk Time: 3hrs 15mins   Distance: 7.5miles/12Km
Start: Norfolk Arms on Ringinglow Road. GR. 291837

1. Leaving from the Norfolk Arms, walk along the lane opposite and approaching Moor Cottage 220yds further on near a bend, continue straight ahead on the wide, rough sandy track keeping a wood on your **RT** to a 5-bar gate. Go through onto high moorland with good views and continue on this wide track known as Houndkirk Road. Continue to a **PF** sign on **RT** pointing **LT** and **RT**. A large broken walled enclosure is on the **LT**.

2. Turn **LT** across the enclosure onto Houndkirk Moor on a wet and narrow path to a post you may see in the distance to the **RT** of Houndkirk Hill. At the post follow the narrow path descending to the main road. Cross with care walking down Whitelow Lane passing farms on **RT** and **LT**.

3. Walk round a **RT** hand bend then 490yds further on, a **LT** hand bend. Follow the road for 500yds keeping a wood on your **LT** then at the top corner of the wood beside the houses, turn **LT** along Newfield Lane keeping the village of Causeway Head on your **RT**. Continue for 1100yds to the junction.

4. Turn **RT** on a footpath along Brickhouse Lane in front of the houses. At next junction 150yds further, turn **RT** opposite the post box onto Causeway Head Lane, walking for 150yds to Parkers Lane on the opposite side.

5. Walk down Parkers Lane to the junction with Limb Lane then turn **LT**. Follow the road, when just after a dip in the road there is a house and a **PB** sign on the **RT**.

6. Turn **RT** along the track, which descends gently, soon to pass a cottage on **LT** and now walking parallel with a stream. A sign states **PB** to Abbeydale and Dore. When you arrive at some wooden 5-bar gates, turn **LT**. A sign states 'horse riding prohibited'.

7. You are now on a winding path through woodland. At a fork in the path keep **LT** towards a house you may see in the distance. You come to a stone wall with a narrow opening between. Go through then straight ahead keeping to the **RT** side of a sports field up to the main road at GR. 310826.

8. Cross with care onto a short semi-circular road at Whirlow Bridge and continue round to the second **PF** on the **LT**, just past a house. A rock face is near the entrance. Walk along the tarmac path skirting around the side of a house and passing a small lake on your **LT**.

9. Stay on the main path as you ascend Limb Valley for 1.2miles on a winding, undulating path, generally keeping parallel with the stream on your **LT**.

10. You eventually come to an open area; turn **LT** now on grass towards Moor Cottage near to where you started. Keep the stream on your **RT** up to the stone steps in front of the cottage, to emerge on the road.

11. Turn **RT** walking for 100yds back to the junction beside the Norfolk Arms.